DRUGS AND DOMESTIC VIOLENCE

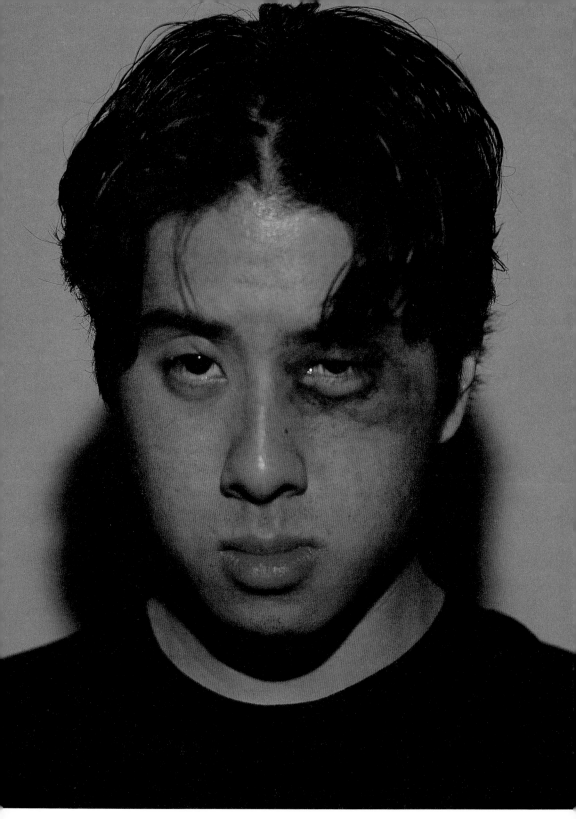

Children and teenagers are most likely to be victims of
family violence.

THE DRUG ABUSE PREVENTION LIBRARY

DRUGS AND DOMESTIC VIOLENCE

Raymond M. Jamiolkowski

THE ROSEN PUBLISHING GROUP, INC.
NEW YORK

To Jenny and David Jamiolkowski
You are the brightest lights in my life.

Published in 1996 by The Rosen Publishing Group, Inc.
29 East 21st Street, New York, NY 10010

First Edition

Library of Congress Cataloging-in-Publication Data

Jamiolkowski, Raymond M.
    Drugs and domestic violence/ Raymond M.
Jamiolkowski. — 1st ed.
      p. cm. — (The drug abuse prevention library)
    Includes bibliographical references and index.
    Summary: Discusses the use of drugs in a domestic
environment, the resulting violence that can occur,
and ways of coping with the situation.
    ISBN 0-8239-2062-3
    1. Drug abuse—United States—Juvenile literature.
2. Family violence—United States—Juvenile literature.
[1. Drug abuse. 2. Family violence.] I. Title.
II. Series.
HV5825.J36   1995
362.82′92—dc20   95-14903
                               CIP
                               AC

Manufactured in the United States of America

Contents

Introduction

Recent studies show that Americans are far more likely to be seriously injured or killed by a family member or a person they know well than they are by a stranger. Violence in families has reached epidemic proportions. The courts are flooded with cases of physical abuse, sexual abuse, and neglect. State agencies responsible for the welfare of children are overworked and understaffed. Meanwhile, cases such as the murder of Nicole Brown Simpson have brought the subject of domestic violence to national attention.

Adding to the increase in domestic violence is an explosion in the use and misuse of drugs. Crack, cocaine, PCP ("angel dust"), amphetamines, steroids, alcohol, and some new designer drugs tend to make users more physically violent. All of these drugs make a person more active and energetic for some period of time. Each time a person uses one of them he experiences a "high" that is followed by a depressing "low."

Other drugs such as marijuana, several prescription drugs, heroin, and some hallucinogens allow people mentally to escape from their everyday lives. While using these drugs people tend to neglect their family, their work, and their own health.

Children and teenagers are most likely to be victims of family violence. Adults "high" on alcohol and drugs often injure their own children simply because they are there. People often use drugs or alcohol at home because their addiction is easier to hide there. As a result of their addiction, some people also abuse their families. Their violence toward family members is hidden at home. Many families who deal with violent members keep it a secret because they are too scared or ashamed to talk about the violence at home.

Drug addiction and alcoholism are diseases that affect every family member. The addict may be a parent or one of the children. But in any case the addict

Taking care of their children is instinctive for most parents.
Using drugs or alcohol can wipe out that instinct.

focuses most or all of his energy on getting or staying high. Addicts don't let anything get in their way. Many lie, cheat, steal, and sometimes even sell their bodies for sex to get the drugs they crave.

In a healthy family each member tries to support, encourage, and protect one another. In a family in which someone is abusing a drug, the drug or alcohol becomes the focus. Family members often deny or cover up the problems. But that only allows the situation to become worse.

Victims of family violence can find help. Thousands of abused and neglected family members escape their attackers each year. There are people who can be trusted and who know how to handle these violent situations in ways that help everyone in the family.

Everyone in a family is affected by one person's addiction, whether that addiction is to drugs or to alcohol.

CHAPTER 1

Drugs in Our Homes

Abuse Through Generations

Darlene had a difficult life. Her parents were divorced when she was young. Her mother felt rejected by her father and became really depressed. Most days when Darlene came home from school her mother was drunk or high on marijuana. The family's only income was the child support her mother received from Darlene's father.

Darlene and her brothers and sisters grew up pretty much on their own. They tried to avoid their mother, who became verbally abusive when she was drunk, screaming that their father had abandoned them, that he was a terrible man, that she hated him and sometimes hated them too. The kids would get

12 *dinner together, eat quickly, then scatter to their separate rooms or to friends' houses.*

When Darlene was 12, her friends started drinking and smoking cigarettes. When they told her how good drinking made them feel, Darlene decided to try it too. Soon she was meeting her friends every weekend to party, drinking until she could barely stand up.

When she was 14, Darlene's best friend dared her to steal some of her mother's pot. Darlene knew where it was kept, and since her mother had usually passed out by dinner, she figured that it would be easy to take. It was. She and her friends made a new habit of raiding her mother's supply. Darlene loved the way she felt when she was high—she didn't care about anything. By the time her sweet sixteenth rolled around, Darlene was buying her own supply nearly every day.

One night, high on pot and three vodka-and-tonics, Darlene decided to have sex with the guy she'd had a crush on for two years. They began to have sex regularly. They rarely practiced safe sex, however. They were both usually too drunk or high to remember condoms or other birth control. By 17, Darlene was pregnant with her first baby, Serina.

About a month after she realized that she was pregnant, Darlene tried to cut back on

People who are high on drugs or alcohol may take their anger or aggression out on anyone who happens to be around, including a younger sibling.

drinking and smoking. When the baby was born, she tried even harder, but it was so difficult. Serina was a low birth-weight baby and didn't sleep through the night. Darlene quickly became frustrated with her. More than once her older brother had caught her screaming at the baby to "shut up or get a slap."

Darlene took Serina to the park with her every day to meet her friends. She left Serina in the carriage while she and her friends smoked pot. One afternoon, Darlene and her friends had just finished a huge joint

13

14 | *and were all feeling great. They decided to go swimming. They ran down to the pond, playing in the water and swimming all afternoon. Darlene forgot one thing, her baby. A few hours later, Darlene went home laughing and joking with her friends.*

A police car was in front of their house. Suddenly remembering her baby, Darlene pushed her way into the house. "My Serina, my baby! What happened to my baby?" Darlene's sisters stared at the floor, but her brother looked her straight in the eye. "You have become worse than Mom. You're lucky someone saw her. The police took Serina to a state home. They want to talk to you about putting your baby in danger."

Drug Abuse and Siblings

Karl Henderson was captain of his school's wrestling team and linebacker for the football team. At 17, he was one of the best athletes in school. His teachers and coaches admired Karl's hard work and determination. Karl was frustrated because scouts from the big colleges seldom came to see his teams compete. He needed to make himself stand out.

Each summer Karl participated in a county weight training program for athletes. Over the years he had made many friends from other towns. One of his best friends was Roger Adams from Cross City.

When Karl arrived at camp this year he noticed that Roger had put on at least thirty pounds—all muscle. Karl asked him how he had done it. Roger answered with a question, "Can you keep a secret?"

Karl was puzzled, "Of course I can!"

Roger told him that he had started to use steroids. The steroids not only made him bigger and stronger, but when he played football he played harder than ever. He told Karl that "for some stupid reason" steroids are illegal, but that in his opinion they made him a better athlete.

Steroids sounded great to Karl. Roger showed him how to inject himself where no one would notice. As Karl used the drug he did become stronger, and he put on about a pound of muscle per week. He also became meaner and less concerned with other people's feelings.

When Karl came back from camp, his family noticed a change. He was bigger and stronger, but he was also angrier. Karl would become irritated at the smallest thing. He argued with his mother over doing his regular chores. When his father told him to treat his mother with respect, he stormed out of the house.

Karl's younger brother, Frank, noticed the

Abuse and neglect often become patterns of family behavior passed down from one generation to another. But it can be stopped.

change as well. Frank and Karl always used to roughhouse together, wrestling or working on football plays. But now Karl played too hard. Frank was bruised in several places.

A few days later they were playing touch football in the yard with a couple of Karl's friends. When Frank caught the football Karl slapped him to the ground. Frank tried to break his fall with his arm, but instead landed on it hard. He lay on the ground with his arm bent at an impossible angle.

Karl stood over him shouting, "You stupid wimp. You should have known better than to play football with us. This is your own fault!"

Drug Use Sexual Abuse

When Kim Walters' father died, she thought that her mother would be sad forever. They both struggled to adjust for the first year, but eventually they got used to their lives without him. They missed him but felt that things must go on.

Kim's mother, Jinny, started dating about two years later. She was very attracted to Ken. He was outgoing, funny, and made a good living as a salesman for an electronics firm. Jinny said that Ken made her laugh for the first time in a long time. Kim was happy for her mother.

Kim did notice that Ken was moody. Most of the time he was full of energy and excitement. One evening, though, he seemed really down and depressed. Kim was surprised, but she didn't think too much about it at the time. After all, she was 15 and went through plenty of mood changes herself.

What Kim didn't know was that Ken's energy and excitement came from cocaine. He always sniffed a little before he came to pick up Jinny. The cocaine gave him a false feeling of confidence. By the end of the evening, however, he would be moody and depressed. Ken would sometimes cover up these feelings by cutting the evening short.

No one has the right to abuse you sexually.

Other times he would simply go into the bathroom and sniff some more cocaine.

After a few months Ken and Jinny became engaged to be married. Kim had come to accept Ken, and he felt like part of their family. She and her mother still did not suspect his drug abuse.

Ken wanted to start a sexual relationship with Jinny. He felt that the time had come to become closer physically, and the cocaine—which he was now using daily—increased his desire for her.

One Saturday they spent the day together.
18 *Ken used more cocaine than usual. As a*

matter of fact, as the day wore on he used up
*his supply. When they got back to her place
Ken felt supercharged. He had never been so
eager for sex in his life. He began coming on
strong to her. But his crudeness turned off
Jinny completely. They argued noisily for a
few minutes; then Ken tried to force himself
on her. Kim walked into the room just as her
mother struggled to push Ken off. Seeing
Kim, Ken shouted, "If I can't have you, I'll
have your daughter."*

*With that he jumped up and ripped off
Kim's shirt. Kim screamed, covered herself,
ran into her bedroom and locked the door
behind her. She had never felt so humiliated
and frightened in her life.*

A person who abuses drugs or alcohol is less rational and has less control over his actions.

CHAPTER 2

An Epidemic of Violence

Violence and neglect are a part of many families' everyday lives. Drugs and alcohol can make a bad situation worse. Most people have an inner voice that reminds them to treat other people, especially family members, well. People also have impulses to strike out when they are angry or frustrated. Drugs and alcohol break down a person's inhibitions. A person who is drunk or high is more likely to give in to the impulse to strike or hurt another person. Often the victim doesn't even know why he was attacked.

One way in which alcoholics and drug users may hurt their families is by **neglect**. Neglect is causing harm to another person for whom you are responsi-

22 | ble by not providing the minimum care that they need to be healthy. Neglect may be **emotional**. People who are addicted to drugs or alcohol are dependent on the drugs or alcohol in order to function. The most important thing in their lives is getting drugs and staying high. Addicts lie, cheat, and steal to get drugs. An addicted parent is unable to meet the family's emotional needs. Children in families with an addict feel that there is no one there for them.

Another form of neglect is **physical** neglect. Failure to provide food, medical care, or shelter is physical neglect. Many families are too poor to afford the best of these, but there are governmental agencies and other groups that can provide free or inexpensive food, medical care, and shelter. Parents who do not take advantage of these programs are neglecting their children. Drugs and alcohol can make parents forget about their responsibilities. Unfortunately, problems of neglect usually become worse with time.

Another way in which alcoholics and drug addicts can hurt their families is by **abuse**. Abuse is actively causing harm to another person. Family members are much more likely to become victims because they are there when the addicted member becomes violent. It is easier to harm a family member in the privacy of one's own home than to attack a stranger in public.

Emotional abuse can cause lasting harm to young people. Constant criticism, negative comments, and insults affect young people deeply. Some victims of emotional abuse react angrily and take out their anger and frustration on other people. Other victims never develop the self-confidence they need to become the best that they can be.

Alcohol, like many drugs, is a depressant. People under the influence of depressants often feel sorry for themselves and take out their self-pity by emotionally abusing people around them.

Physical abuse is harming someone by hitting, punching, squeezing, biting, or using a weapon. Victims of physical abuse receive bruises, cuts, broken bones, cigarette burns, chemical burns, scalds from boiling water, bites, and worse. Being locked in a small space for long periods of time is also a type of physical abuse. Many victims of abuse are embarrassed to ask for assistance, but they need to have the courage to find people who can help.

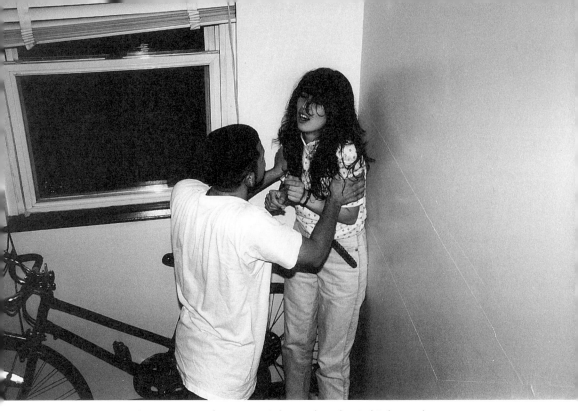

A person can become violent when he is high on drugs or drunk on alcohol.

All states in the U.S. and Canadian provinces have laws forbidding physical abuse. Police, social workers, teachers, doctors, and clergy (priests, pastors, rabbis, imams, etc.) are often trained to help victims of abuse. The laws are written to protect victims, but abused family members need to tell someone before it is too late.

Alcohol and other drugs take away our inhibitions. People high on drugs can lose control easily and can seriously injure or even kill another person by physically abusing them.

Another form of violence in the family

is **sexual abuse**. Any sexual activity between a child and another family member can be called incest. It is not limited to sexual intercourse. If a member of your family touches your private areas (genitals, breasts, or buttocks), exposes their own private areas, makes comments suggesting sexual situations, or forces you to watch or be a part of pornographic pictures, that is incest too.

Users of cocaine and many designer drugs often believe that these drugs increase their sexual feeling. These drug abusers are more likely to sexually abuse family members.

Victims of sexual abuse are usually fearful of telling anyone about their abuse. Sexual abuse often makes its victims feel dirty, used, and worthless. Sometimes victims feel that they caused the abuse. This is never true.

Another form of abuse that can result from drug use is abuse of unborn babies. The recent dramatic increase in the use of cocaine, especially crack cocaine, has led to babies being born addicted. Babies born addicted to cocaine suffer lifelong effects of their mothers' abuse. They are smaller than other babies. They suffer the pain of withdrawal from the drug during

26 | the first days of their lives. These babies cry loudly and often and are nearly impossible to soothe. They often grow up unable to fit in well with other people. They frequently develop behavior problems and are far more likely to have a learning disability.

Likewise, babies born to alcoholic mothers may have fetal alcohol syndrome (FAS). As a result of their mother's intake of alcohol while pregnant, their own development suffers. They are born with a lowered intelligence and poor muscle control. This can affect everything from fine tasks like handwriting and drawing to basic tasks such as running, throwing, and catching.

Laws are being enacted to test newborns for the presence of illegal drugs in their systems. Mothers of cocaine or heroin babies may have their child removed and may face charges of child abuse. Lawmakers hope that these laws will encourage pregnant women to stop their drug use.

CHAPTER 3

Chemicals of Abuse

*V*iolence in families can take many forms. People under the influence of drugs tend to act in particular ways. To cope with an addicted family member in a violent home, it is important first to understand what is happening. Understanding the effects of different drugs will help.

Alcohol

The most commonly abused drug is alcohol. People have been using and abusing alcohol for a long time. Alcoholism is a serious disease. An alcoholic's life is centered on drinking.

In some ways, alcoholism is harder to treat than addiction to other drugs

27

28 because alcohol is legal to use. Many alcoholics believe that they really do not have a problem. Yet when an alcoholic abuses or neglects his family, a serious problem exists.

Alcohol produces a drunken "high." When people are drunk they feel happy, silly, and carefree. Often they lose their inhibitions and do things that they would not do if they were sober.

There are many prices to be paid for the high. One is that when a person has been drinking, his judgment is impaired. Driving, crossing a busy highway, swimming, or other activities are much more dangerous to a person who has been drinking alcohol. The alcohol makes a person feel that he can say or do whatever comes into his mind.

A person who is intoxicated is not only a danger to himself. If he drives, possesses a weapon, or simply becomes angry, he becomes a danger to everyone he encounters. Emotional, physical, or even sexual abuse are often the result for family members as well.

Another price to be paid for becoming drunk is that people tend to suffer a "hangover" the next day. During a hangover a person develops a bad headache, nausea, and poor coordination. Regret and mild depression are usually part of the hangover. A person suffering from a hangover is often crabby, angry, and irritable. Family members usually learn to avoid an alcoholic parent when he or she is hungover.

Alcoholism, like other drug addictions, is a disease. It does not go away on its own. Like other addicts, the alcoholic needs professional medical and psychological help. Family members cannot cause another person to drink. Alone they cannot get him to stop either.

Prescription Drugs

Each year doctors prescribe millions of drugs to their patients. Some of these drugs are to help people sleep better, lose weight, remain calm, think more clearly, get rid of pain, behave appropriately, and more. All can be very helpful if they are used properly. Many people, however, abuse these drugs.

Overuse of prescription drugs can lead to addiction. **Painkillers** will get rid of pain if the correct amount is used. If too many painkillers are taken the user experiences a high, but puts his health in danger.

Tranquilizers are the most commonly

30 used prescription drugs. Their purpose is to calm people down so that they feel less frustration, anxiety, or anger. Over-use of tranquilizers can make a person dependent on them.

People who are usually sad, gloomy, and negative and who think frequently of suicide may suffer from depression. In this case, doctors sometimes prescribe **antidepressants**. These drugs can have serious side effects if the patient does not receive therapy at the same time to try to uncover the things in his life that are making him unhappy.

Although they are legal, prescription drugs cause problems in two ways. First, a person dependent on prescription drugs needs to obtain a source of supply. A doctor must not give out prescriptions for more and more of the same drug if the patient is not getting better. So the drug-dependent person uses up time and energy persuading new doctors to prescribe the drug or finding an illegal source for the drug.

A second problem is that the drug-dependent person relies on the drug to take away day-to-day problems. Instead of solving problems, the drug simply makes them easier to ignore. This can lead to emotional and physical neglect or abuse of family members.

Marijuana

Many people consider marijuana a harmless substance, but it can be devastating for a family.

Marijuana users feel a high while under its influence. They may feel silly and funny. Other times they may simply be very calm or mellow. Marijuana seems like an escape from the difficulties of everyday life.

Most drugs that people abuse are water-soluble. That means that the drug passes out of the body through urine in a matter of hours after being used. Marijuana, however, is fat-soluble. That means that it dissolves in the fat of a person's body. The chemicals in marijuana stay in the body for months after use. For this reason, even after the high wears off, the marijuana is still there making a person calmer, but less likely to work hard for a goal and see things through to the end.

Marijuana users very seldom become physically violent. However, they are much more likely to neglect their families physically, emotionally, and financially.

Studies show that smoking marijuana can affect the user's long-term memory.

They may use marijuana to escape and may not care about what is happening to the rest of their family.

Cocaine

For many years cocaine was called the "champagne of drugs." It was very expensive and was mainly used by wealthy people such as rock stars and movie actors. In the past few years a new form of cocaine has been introduced: crack. Crack is an inexpensive, one-dose form of cocaine. A vial of crack costs about ten dol-

Drug addicts often resort to stealing from family members and others to support their habits.

34 | lars compared to hundreds of dollars for powdered cocaine. When crack is smoked it enters the body in a matter of seconds and produces a very strong high. This high lasts from five to ten minutes and is then followed by a crash. Most crack users desperately seek to get rid of the crash by smoking more crack.

Crack is one of the most addictive drugs ever known. Crack addicts commonly steal, lie, cheat, and even sell their own bodies sexually for money to buy more crack. Gangs and street criminals often control the sale of crack. This leads to greater crime in a neighborhood both by the dealers and by the addicts trying to obtain more money to buy the drug.

People may become extremely violent while under the influence of crack. Several murders of family members have been associated with its use. Cocaine also tends to release sexual impulses. This can lead to sexual abuse of family members.

Crack relaxes sexual inhibitions and may make users less concerned about using birth control. And addicts sometimes trade sex for drugs. As a result, each year 200,000 babies are born addicted to crack or cocaine. These children will carry the effects of their mother's drug abuse with them all their lives.

Amphetamines

Another type of drug that is widely abused is **amphetamines.** Amphetamines were originally developed to give people more energy, to help them stay alert and be able to concentrate for longer periods of time, and as an aid in losing weight. Unfortunately, amphetamines are very disruptive to the natural patterns of rest and activity of the human body. People abusing amphetamines may stay awake for long periods of time. After a while they are unable to think clearly, concentrate, and make reliable decisions. Yet the drug will not allow them to fall asleep. People using amphetamines can become unpredictably violent after long use.

Hallucinogens

During the 1960s many writers and artists experimented with hallucinogenic drugs. Some believed that drugs such as LSD, PCP, mescaline, and psilocybin (magic mushrooms) made them more creative. Users like Dr. Timothy Leary

36 | suggested that people try the drugs to help them understand themselves.

These drugs have turned out to be very dangerous. Users of hallucinogens believe that they are seeing things that are not really there. Sometimes the hallucinations are colorful and beautiful. Other times they are bizarre and frightening. Some people have jumped out of windows to their death in order to escape imaginary attackers or because they thought that they could fly. Other users have seen hallucinations so frightening that their minds shut out the rest of the world while they lie as if in a coma.

Hallucinogens are dangerous because they are so unpredictable. People using these drugs may act in "crazy" ways because of the visions that they see in their mind. These drugs are not physically addictive but can lead to serious violence in a family.

Narcotics

The strongest pain-killing drugs are called narcotics. These drugs include Demerol, codeine, morphine, and heroin. All are made from the opium poppy. All have or had medical use but are highly addictive and widely abused.

Many narcotics addicts are people who have suffered great pain through an accident or illness. Doctors may have prescribed the drug to relieve the pain, but the user developed an addiction. Other narcotics addicts simply move from alcohol and marijuana to cocaine and then finally to heroin, which is considered to be a more "serious" drug. Some crack addicts use narcotics to end the crashing low that follows their crack high. This combination is often fatal.

Narcotics abuse combines the worst of other addictions. The narcotics addict neglects everything and everyone important to him in order to get more narcotics. Many narcotics addicts turn to crime to support their habit.

Another problem with narcotics is that these drugs are generally injected into the body with a hypodermic needle. These needles may be difficult to obtain, so addicts often share them. If one of the users has HIV (human immunodeficiency virus), AIDS (acquired immunodeficiency syndrome), or hepatitis, the disease can be spread through blood left in the needle.

Steroids

In our society people feel a strong need

When abused, narcotics can cause the user to neglect everything around him.

to compete. This is even more true on the athletic fields. Competitors look for that little edge that will help their team to win. Some athletes turn to steroids to give them that edge.

Steroids are drugs that promote growth in the human body. Doctors often prescribe steroids to decrease the time that it takes for an injury to heal. Athletes using steroids increase muscle mass and strength and are able to compete longer. But when steroids are abused, there are some serious side effects.

Steroids can lead to dramatic and sometimes violent mood swings, high blood pressure, kidney malfunction, liver damage, skin tumors, and contraction of the sex organs. Steroids often cause bone growth to stop. The result is that users fail to reach the height to which they would have grown otherwise. Steroid use is also associated with cancer.

The angry, aggressive behavior that is a result of steroid abuse is a serious concern for families. Steroid users are at risk for serious health problems for themselves in the future, but they may inflict harm on their families today.

Designer Drugs

One hundred years ago all the drugs mentioned in this chapter were legal to possess and use. As people became aware of their harmful effects, laws were made to control their use. As new drugs are developed and distributed, new laws are made to control the new drugs. Designer drugs are new drugs made by people with some chemical and pharmacy expertise. These new drugs are designed to make their producers a profit and to stay one step ahead of the law.

Some of the designer drugs are

40 stronger and longer lasting than anything that occurs naturally. A new drug called "ice" can keep a user awake and energetic for three to five days at a time. Unfortunately, the crashing low that follows the high has led to many suicides.

Other designer drugs combine the effects of two different drugs. MDMA or "ecstasy" is supposed to produce a long-lasting mellow high. A side effect of long-term use of MDMA seems to be brain damage.

There is no quality control in the production of designer drugs. Many deaths and mental disturbances have resulted from the slightest of errors in the drug preparation procedures.

As technology improves, these designer drugs will become more and more common, more potent, and more harmful to families.

CHAPTER 4

Addicted Families

A drug addict is a person whose body chemistry depends on a drug in order to function. Drug addicts experience discomfort, depression, and sometimes severe physical pain when they are unable to obtain the drug that their body needs. Some people seem to be addiction-prone. The first time they use a drug they are hooked. They can never seem to get enough and are miserable unless they are high. Some drugs are more addictive than others. Anyone who tries crack cocaine becomes addicted quickly and easily. On the other hand hallucinogens, while they are extremely dangerous drugs, are not physically addictive at all.

Some people develop an addiction over

42 | time. They may use a drug with little effect. After using the same drug a number of times they are unable to stop using it. Nicotine is addictive in this way. People who smoke tobacco are often addicted to the nicotine before they even know it.

People who are addicted to drugs suffer from **withdrawal symptoms** when they stop using the drug. They may feel depressed, frightened, and anxious. They may throw up, shake, and break into cold sweats. Frightening hallucinations and delusions sometimes occur during withdrawal. It may take weeks or even months before their body chemistry returns to normal.

After going through all this, a drug addict is still not "cured." The addict still desires the drug and needs to struggle to avoid using it again. That's why drug addiction is almost impossible to break alone. Addicts need support while going through withdrawal and afterward to remind them how important it is to avoid using drugs.

Many people do not think of alcohol as a drug, but **alcoholism** is simply one type of drug addiction. As a matter of fact, alcohol is the most widely abused drug in the world. An alcoholic depends

Recovering alcoholics and drug addicts often suffer from withdrawal symptoms, which may include the shakes, nausea, and vomiting.

Every member of a family is affected by an addict's behavior. This behavior is often angry or aggressive.

on alcohol in exactly the same way as any other drug addict. Alcoholics experience withdrawal symptoms if they suddenly stop drinking, and alcoholics, like all other addicts, never fully recover from their addiction.

Drug addicts and alcoholics do not carry the addiction alone. Families of addicts are affected as well. Addiction affects everyone who loves or cares about the addict.

Denial

A leading contributor to continued alco-

holism or drug addiction in a family is
denial. The alcoholic or drug abuser
claims that he is not using drugs, that he
only uses drugs once in a while, that he
can handle the drugs, that drugs are not
affecting work or school, that he "found"
some money and used it to buy drugs.
Drug addicts lie, cheat, and steal to get
more drugs. Often they believe their own
lies. They think that they are handling the
drugs and that they are still in control of
their own lives.

Family members may also deny the
drug use. Even when it is obvious that
the addict is using alcohol or drugs,
spouses and children often refuse to believe it. They tell themselves: "He's under
a lot of pressure," "She was just curious,"
"Things are going to get better and he'll
stop," "It was my fault that he hit me," or
"I deserved all the terrible names she
called me." All of these statements are
examples of denial, and all of them are
lies.

Sometimes spouses and children are
embarrassed about the drug use. Sometimes they are afraid that the police will
arrest the user and send him to jail. Actu-
ally, programs that help people to recover
from addiction are not particularly inter-

Without meaning to, family members sometimes help an abusive addict to continue abusive behavior by not talking about it to anyone.

ested in sending addicted people to jail. They only want to help them to stop using alcohol and drugs. It is essential that drug users get professional help. An addict who continues to use drugs regularly is much more likely to end up in jail, seriously injured, or dead.

Enabling

Another condition that allows alcoholics and drug addicts to continue in their use is enabling. Enabling means that the family acts in ways that make it easier for a person to continue addictive behavior. If a family member physically or sexually abuses someone else in the family, that abuse needs to be reported. To keep abuse secret is to enable the abuse to continue. School counselors, social workers, doctors, clergy, and child welfare agencies can all be helpful in these cases. Many families afflicted by drugs and violence suffer in silence, allowing the abuse to continue.

In some families everyone tries to take stress and pressure off of the addict. They think that if everyone is patient and kind the addict will no longer feel that he needs to use drugs and will stop on his own. This approach never works. It simply allows the addict to continue to use drugs hassle-free. Drug abuse should not be tolerated. Brothers, sisters, children, and spouses all need to tell the drug abuser "No!"

Codependency

It is easy for members of an addict's family to become codependents. A codependent is someone who has allowed his own life to be changed by someone else's addiction. It is much easier for an addict to continue his use if he has a family of codependents to make excuses

By cleaning up after or making excuses for an addict or an alcoholic, you are enabling him or her to continue with his or her addiction.

for him, cover up for him, lie to keep him out of trouble, and lend him money when he says that he needs it.

It is important for family members to avoid or unlearn codependent behavior. Getting help for yourself is a healthy way for you to deal with someone else's addiction. Telling the truth and finding trained people to talk to is a good first step. Refusing to deny or enable are the best ways

to help an addict.

CHAPTER 5

Coping in a Violent Home

*C*oping with family violence does not mean simply hanging on and hoping that everything will turn out okay. Coping with violence means taking the steps necessary to keep yourself and other family members safe. These steps usually begin with talking to your family to see how they feel about drug use, alcohol use, and violence in your home.

The second step is to talk to someone at school, at church, in the community, on a help hotline, or at Alateen. This will help you to decide whether you need help, what kind of help is needed, and what steps to take.

The third step is to make a plan in-

50 volving your entire family to stop the addiction and violence. This may take the form of an intervention, a stay at a family shelter, or some other organized plan.

The fourth and final step is to put the plan into action. This step takes courage, patience, and the support of other people. It is the beginning of the family's recovery from drugs and violence.

Finding Help at School

It is usually best to talk to someone outside of the family to decide if you really need help. School counselors, social workers, school nurses, or student assistance coordinators all are good people to whom to turn. If you think that your family is dangerously violent or that a family member's addiction is hurting you, sit down privately with one of these people and ask his opinion. Make sure that you tell him all of the important facts. His advice can be only as good as the information that you give him.

In most states school personnel must report child abuse to a state or local child welfare agency. This should not make you hesitate to speak to any of them. It only means that if your situation is dangerous to you, they will take action to help you.

You can find help and advice at your place of worship.

Church, Temple, or Mosque

Another place to find help is at your place of worship. Priests, ministers, rabbis, imams, and the youth workers associated with them usually receive training to help young people and families deal with addiction and violence. Not only will you find help and a listening ear, but their services are nearly always free.

Community Resources

Each community has different groups to assist families in need. Some have established family shelters. These are places, usually a house, where abused families

51

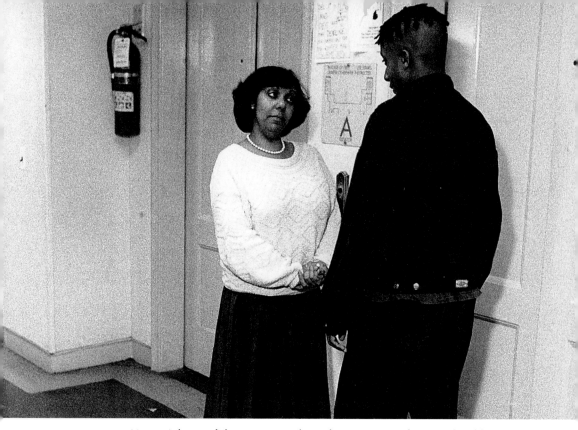

You might confide in a trusted teacher or counselor at school.

can go to escape the violence in the home. The family can be protected temporarily from the abuser while they take steps to deal with the violence. Usually a temporary escape from the home is enough to help the family stand up against the drugs and violence.

The YMCA and YWCA are organizations established in many communities to support the healthy growth of young people. Many have wonderful programs designed to give teenagers the tools that they need to grow up into healthy adults. The national organizations have developed programs to curb physical, emotional, and sexual violence.

Many police departments have developed programs to help young people. Many departments have social workers or officers on staff assigned to work with youth and talk to anyone who requests it. A program called D.A.R.E. (Drug Awareness Resistance Education) has been introduced in many schools. These police officers are trained in the best ways to help families undergoing problems with drugs.

Other resources are available in most communities. Look in the yellow pages of your phone book under alcoholism, drug addiction, mental health, psychologists, social workers, or social service agencies for organizations in your community.

Hotlines

Another source of help are telephone crisis lines or hotlines. These are staffed by caring people who are trained to help in an emergency. The disadvantage of talking to hotline workers is that they don't really know you and may not be able to understand your situation fully. An advantage of hotlines, though, is that they are strictly confidential. Hotline

54 | workers cannot take action unless you tell them who you are and where you live. Several helpful hotline numbers are listed in the back of this book. In an extreme emergency in most communities you can simply call the police at 911.

Alateen and Al-Anon

Just as Alcoholics Anonymous is the largest and most effective program for helping addicts recover from alcoholism and drug abuse, Alateen has proved to be the best program for helping teenagers and preteens to deal with addiction in their families. All of the participants in Alateen have been hurt by the addiction of someone close to them. Alateen can help teenagers learn to stop enabling the addict and how to avoid violence at home.

Al-Anon is an organization for spouses and adult family members who are affected by addiction. In a family with an addicted parent, it is most effective if the children and teenagers join Alateen while the parent who is not addicted joins Al-Anon. In single-parent families, families in which both parents are addicted, or families in which the parent who is not addicted denies that there is a problem, joining Alateen alone will still help quite a bit.

Recovery

When an addict makes a decision to stop using alcohol or drugs he begins a process called **recovery**. Some people are forced to stop using drugs by hospitalization or being put in jail. They may stop using drugs and even go through withdrawal, but they have not begun to recover until they decide that they want to end their drug use. No one can make that decision for another person. That is why it is so difficult for a family to help.

Often families conduct an **intervention**. An intervention is a meeting of important loved ones and family members in the addict's life under the direction of a trained addiction counselor. During the intervention everyone tells the addict how they feel about his drug or alcohol use, how it affects them, and how much they care about him. The intervention can be a powerful means of assisting an addict in his decision to end his drug usage.

Most addicts begin recovery with some type of hospital program. They may be an inpatient, meaning that they live at the hospital for a period of time. Most programs today are outpatient, meaning that the addict comes in for treatment during the day but returns home at night. When

56 | an addict has been violently abusing family members, the court may order inpatient hospitalization until psychologists are convinced that the family is safe.

Following hospitalization, addicts continue to recover for the rest of their lives. **Alcoholics Anonymous** is the largest organization dedicated to assisting alcoholics and other drug addicts during their recovery. **Narcotics Anonymous** and **Cocaine Anonymous** are two other organizations that have helped thousands through recovery. All of these programs are known as twelve-step programs because they follow the twelve-step recovery process of Alcoholics Anonymous. You can find these organizations in the yellow pages in your phone book.

Violence in the family is a scary thing. It means that some kind of abuse is happening in a place that is supposed to be safe and secure. You can't control what family you were born into, or even how the members of that family act. You *can* control how you deal with the way they treat you. There are plenty of places to go for help. All you have to do is ask.

Glossary
Explaining New Words

addiction   Compulsion to use a drug.

AIDS (acquired immunodeficiency syndrome)   Fatal disease of the immune system believed to be caused by a virus and transmitted by the exchange of body fluids through sexual activity or sharing of infected needles.

Al-Anon   Support group for adults who are affected by someone else's alcohol (or other drug) use.

Alateen   Support group for young people who are affected by someone else's alcohol (or other drug) use.

Alcoholics Anonymous (AA)   Support group for chemically dependent people.

alcoholism   Illness of people who are dependent on alcohol.

amphetamines   Drugs that speed up the central nervous system.

chemical dependence   Strong feeling of need that causes people to keep taking a drug even when it is harmful.

codependent   Someone who has

58 allowed his own life to be changed by someone else's addiction.

compulsion Uncontrolled need to do something repeatedly.

controlled substance Any drug or chemical legally available only under special circumstances.

denial Unwillingness to admit the truth.

dysfunctional family Family in which some members are not having their needs for safety, belonging, growth, or self-esteem met.

emotional abuse Psychological damage caused by another person's words or actions.

enabling Acting in ways that make it easier for a person to continue addictive behavior.

hallucinogens Drugs that make you see things that aren't there or hallucinate.

high Temporary feeling of strength or pleasure, often induced by drugs.

impulse Sudden inclination to act, usually, without fore thought.

inhibitions Internal voice telling you to control your impulses.

physical abuse Injury or damage to a person inflicted by someone entrusted to care for him.

prescription drugs Drugs that can be
bought at a drugstore with permission
of a doctor.

sexual abuse Any unwanted sexual
activity including touching of private
areas, sexual comments, exposure to
pornography, and sexual intercourse.

steroids Controlled substances used
illegally for building body mass and
muscle bulk and for increasing athletic
speed.

substance abuse Use of illegal drugs,
or use of alcohol or prescription drugs
in a way that they were not intended,
all to excess.

tranquilizer Prescription drug designed
to make people calmer and less
anxious.

Help List

In the United States

Al-Anon or Alateen
P.O. Box 862
Midtown Station
New York, NY 10018-0862

Alcoholics Anonymous
1-800-662-HELP

Cocaine Help Line
1-800-COCAINE

Drug and Alcohol Hotline
1-800-252-6465

Narcotics Anonymous
World Service Office
16155 Wyandotte Street
Van Nuys, CA 91406

Prevention Crisis Hotline
1-800-9-FRIEND

Toughlove
P.O. Box 1069
Doylestown, PA 18901

Yellow Pages of the Telephone Book:
Drug Abuse, Counseling, Social Services

School
Counselors, social workers, school nurse,
health services, student assistance
coordinator

Community

Church, synagogue, or mosque, YMCA, YWCA

Support Groups
Check the bulletin board in your school's nurses office or counseling office for more information

In Canada

Alcoholics Anonymous
#502, Intergroup Office
234 Enlington Avenue E.
Toronto, ON M4P 1K5
416-487-5591

Alcohol and Drug Dependency Information and Counseling Services (ADDICS)
#2, 2471 1/2 Portage Avenue
Winnipeg, MB R3J 0N6
204-831-1999

Institute for the Prevention of Child Abuse
25 Spadina Road
Toronto, DN M5R 259
(416) 921-3151

Narcotics Anonymous
P.O. Box 7500
Station A
Toronto, ON M5W 1P9
416-691-9519

Ontario Coalition Rape Crisis Center
(705) 268-8381

Ottawa Sexual Assault Centre Hotline
(613) 234-2266

Peterborough Rape Crisis Centre Hotline
(705) 876-4444

For Further Reading

Edwards, Gabrielle I. *Drugs on Your Streets*, rev. ed. New York: Rosen Publishing Group, 1994.

Martin, Jo, and Clendenon, Kelly. *Drugs and the Family*. New York: Chelsea House Publishers, 1988.

McCormick, Michael. *Designer-Drug Abuse*. New York: Franklin Watts, 1989.

McFarland, Rhoda. *Drugs and Your Parents*, rev. ed. New York: Rosen Publishing Group, 1993.

Schniderman, Nancy, and Hurwitz, Sue. rev. ed. *Drugs and Birth Defects*. New York: Rosen Publishing Group, 1995.

Seixas, Judith S. *Living with a Parent Who Takes Drugs*. New York: Greenwillow Books, 1989.

Index

About the Author

Raymond M. Jamiolkowski received a B.A. in elementary education and an M.A. in guidance and counseling from Northern Illinois University, DeKalb. He taught grades two, five, and six, and has since worked as a guidance counselor.

Mr. Jamiolkowsi lives in Naperville, Illinois, with his wife, Mel, his daughter, Jenny, and his son, David.

Photo Credits

Cover, p. 2 by Michael Brandt; p. 10 by Katherine Hsu; pp. 8, 13 by Yung-Hee Chia, p. 24 by Maria Moreno; pp. 44, 52 by Lauren Piperno; p. 46 by Marcus Shaffer; p. 51 by Kim Sonsky/ Matthew Baumann; all other photos by Kathleen McClancy.